Visual Geography Series®

CHILE

...in Pictures

Prepared by
Nathan A. Haverstock

Lerner Publications Company
Minneapolis

Courtesy of Inter-American Development Bank

Eighty percent of the employees are women at this textile plant in Santiago.

This is an all-new edition of the Visual Geography Series. Previous editions have been published by Sterling Publishing Company, New York City, and some of the original textual information has been retained. New photographs, maps, charts, captions, and updated information have been added. The text has been entirely reset in 10/12 Century Textbook.

LIBRARY OF CONGRESS CATALOGING-IN-PUBLICATION DATA

Haverstock, Nathan A.
  Chile in pictures.

  (Visual geography series)
  Rev. ed. of: Chile in pictures / prepared by Lois Bianchi.
  Includes index.
  Summary: Describes the geography, history, government, economy, culture, and people of the South American country whose narrow land area extends half the length of the continent.
  1. Chile. [1. Chile] I. Bianchi, Lois. Chile in pictures. II. Series: Visual geography series (Minneapolis, Minn.)
  F3058.H33 1988   983   87-2742
  ISBN 0-8225-1809-0 (lib. bdg.)

International Standard Book Number: 0-8225-1809-0
Library of Congress Catalog Card Number: 87-2742

VISUAL GEOGRAPHY SERIES ®

Publisher
Harry Jonas Lerner
Associate Publisher
Nancy M. Campbell
Executive Series Editor
Mary M. Rodgers
Assistant Series Editor
Gretchen Bratvold
Editorial Assistant
Nora W. Kniskern
Illustrations Editors
Nathan A. Haverstock
Karen A. Sirvaitis
Consultants/Contributors
Dr. Ruth F. Hale
Nathan A. Haverstock
Sandra K. Davis
Designer
Jim Simondet
Cartographer
Carol F. Barrett
Indexer
Sylvia Timian
Production Manager
Richard J. Hannah

Independent Picture Service

A group of children parade home after a religious ceremony, followed by family and friends.

Acknowledgments

Title page photo courtesy of L'Enc Matte.

Elevation contours adapted from *The Times Atlas of the World,* seventh comprehensive edition (New York: Times Books, 1985).

Julio Provoste *(left)*, who heads a company that builds fishing vessels, discusses the possibility of a loan to increase production with Gustavo Canas, a loan officer for the Inter-American Development Bank.

Contents

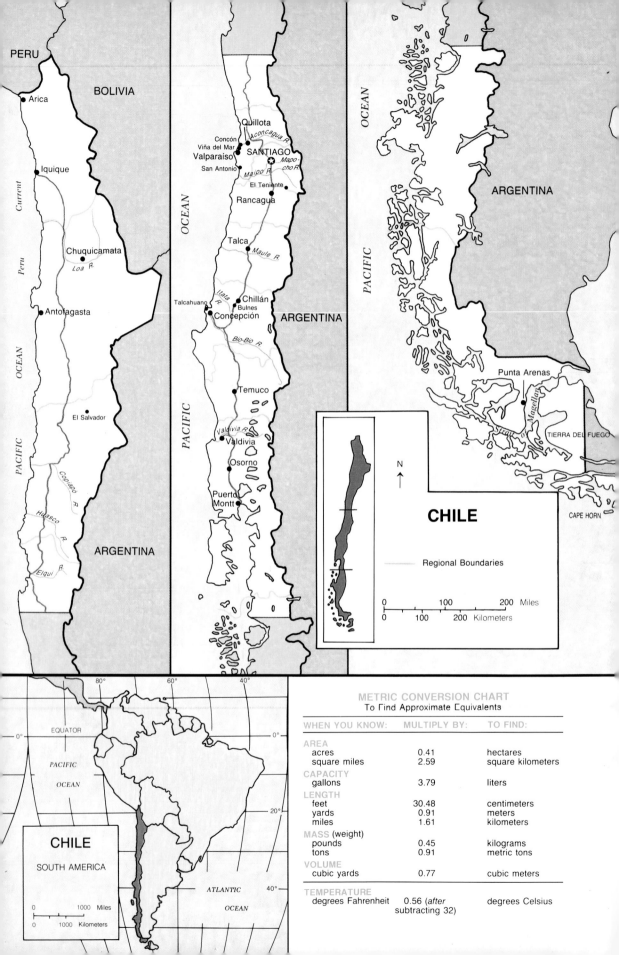

Photo by Don Irish

Although the University of Chile is a state-run institution, students on campus frequently protest against Chile's military regime. Political parties have been banned by the junta, and other forms of opposition are not tolerated.

Introduction

Since 1973 Chileans have endured a military dictatorship, which those in power claim is the price of protecting the nation from Communism. For Chileans, this period has been difficult, and they are anxious for a return to democratic elections, scheduled for late 1989.

Because student protests have been the only tolerated form of opposition under military rule, young people frequently demonstrate their political beliefs during their years on campus. Many Chileans realize that, despite economic progress, deeply rooted differences still exist between the nation's rich and poor. Some students advocate an economic system based on capitalism (private ownership), which appeals to those of inherited wealth. Others support socialism and believe that inequalities can be eliminated only if the state controls and distributes the fruits of the nation's labor and natural resources. Both groups of students are influenced by the example of governments in Europe, such as West Germany, which have democratic forms of socialism.

The differences among the nation's citizens were so strongly demonstrated at voting booths after World War II that national elections failed to produce clear-cut winners. In keeping with Chile's constitution, when no candidate won a majority

5

Mountain-ringed Santiago is the seat of the government of the Republic of Chile.

(over half of the total votes), congress certified the person who received the most votes as the winner.

In 1970 the Chilean congress appointed Salvador Allende—who won just 36 percent of the popular vote—as the new president. A Marxist (someone who follows the socialist system developed by Karl Marx), Allende moved quickly to nationalize the companies that provided the bulk of Chile's wealth, causing domestic and international concern. Some people feared that Allende was determined to make Chile a Communist state.

In response to that fear—and with the support of the U.S. Central Intelligence Agency (CIA)—Chile's military leaders staged a violent coup in 1973. Allende died during the overthrow, but it has not been determined whether he was killed by the generals or committed suicide. Several thousand Chileans—those who the military feared did not support the new government—were killed or driven into exile.

At the time most Chileans seemed willing to tolerate military rule as a necessity

The Cathedral of Santiago is the focus of Chilean Roman Catholicism—the principal religion of the country.

to avoid civil war. The Chilean economy, which had been badly shaken under Allende, revived under the direction of the new head of state, General Augusto Pinochet. In September 1980 Chileans approved, by a two-thirds majority, a new constitution that provided for the gradual restoration of democracy. Chileans who had been forced into exile or who had suffered abuse under the military rule viewed the election with skepticism, fearing that the military did not really intend to put together a democratic form of government.

Nevertheless, in late 1988 Chileans took the next step toward democracy. They voted against giving General Pinochet an eight-year term as president. Although Pinochet lost the election, some Chileans question whether the military will give up control in the presidential and parliamentary elections to be held in December 1989.

A 1960 earthquake in Concepción deformed warehouses and rail lines in Puerto Montt – over 300 miles away. Earthquakes occur frequently in Chile. The most severe tremors struck in 1906, 1939, 1960, and 1970.

Much of Chile's land is mountainous. The country features both low, coastal ranges and rugged, snowcapped Andean peaks, which stretch the length of the South American continent and form Chile's border with Argentina.

1) The Land

The Republic of Chile stretches between the towering Andes and the Pacific Ocean. With 292,257 square miles of territory, Chile is nearly twice the size of California. The country takes its name from the Indian word *chilli*, which means "where the land ends." True to its name, Chile is the southernmost nation of South America. More than 20 times longer than it is wide, Chile is a land of rugged beauty.

Boundaries

Chile's boundaries with Peru and Bolivia to the north and with Argentina to the east are formed by the Andes, whose snowcapped peaks are highest in the northern half of the country. The country shares with Argentina its highest peak, Ojos del Salado, which at 22,539 feet is the second highest mountain in the Western Hemisphere.

Mountains cover approximately one-third of Chile's land surface and isolate the country from its neighbors. The nation's average width from west to east is only about 100 miles, while from north to south the country stretches for 2,650 miles. Ports and inlets and, toward the southern tip of the country, numerous islands dot the Pacific coastline.

Chile also owns some islands in the Pacific far from the mainland. These include the Juan Fernández Islands, 450 miles west of Santiago, where Alexander Selkirk was marooned from 1704 to 1709. Selkirk served as the real-life model for the fictional character Robinson Crusoe, in a novel by Daniel Defoe.

Located about 2,000 miles west of Santiago, Easter Island is the site of an ancient Polynesian culture that is shrouded in mystery. Acquired by Chile in 1888, the island is administered as part of the province of Valparaíso. Most of its 2,000 inhabitants are Polynesians. Their ancestors carved more than 600 huge, humanlike figures from the stone of an extinct volcano located on the southwestern tip of the island. Why they carved these figures and how the ancient peoples raised them to an upright position are questions that remain unanswered.

The Northern Desert

From the Peruvian border in the north to the Aconcagua River, a distance of about

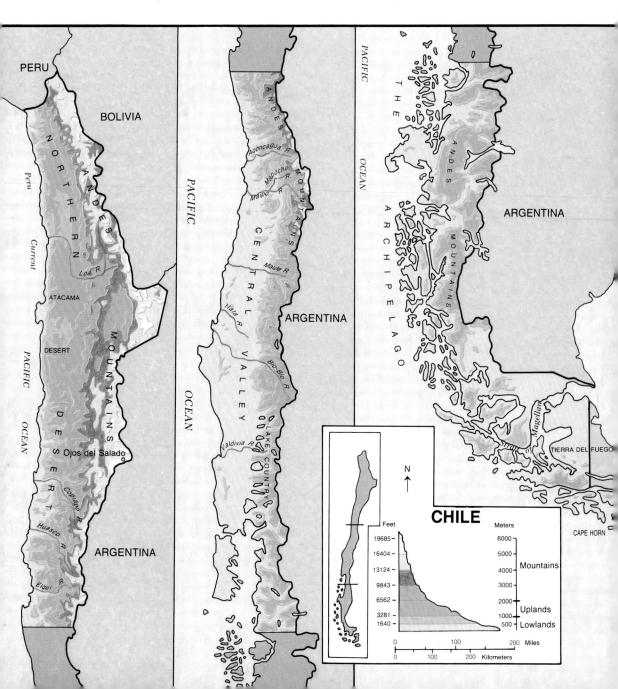

The people of Easter Island carved approximately 600 stone figures, or *moai*. These huge sculptures—which stand as high as 40 feet—are thought to represent the islanders' ancestors, who were of Polynesian origin. The figures were built larger and larger until about 300 years ago, when all work stopped because the Polynesian population was devastated by slave raiding and by disease. This statue—with a typically long face—has been moved to Viña del Mar, where it overlooks the sea.

1,000 miles, lies a bleak and barren region that is mostly flat, with some arid valleys and treeless mountains. This northern desert is a treasure-house of minerals.

This dreary and forbidding place has played a very an important role in Chile's history. Beginning in the nineteenth century, its rich deposits of nitrate—a natural fertilizer—helped farmers in other nations to feed the world's rapidly growing population. Other minerals from the region—including gold, silver, copper, nickel, lead,

With annual rainfall averaging only 0.5 inches, the Atacama Desert in the extreme north of Chile is one of the driest regions in the world. Periodic heavy summer rains and melting winter snows cause occasional flooding.

The copper mine at the town of El Salvador exploits the rich mineral deposits underneath the desert sands.

and manganese—have also been mined as raw materials for overseas industries.

The desert is largely devoid of vegetation. Notable exceptions are the occasional green oases (fertile areas) created by costly irrigation works, where fruits and barley are grown to feed miners and their families. High wages and new towns built by the mining companies attracted settlers to the area.

Covering nearly one-third of Chile, the northern desert is dominated by the Atacama Desert, one of the driest places on earth. No vegetation grows in this region, and rain clouds rarely pass overhead. Rail lines built to carry ore from the mines to seaports cross the desert in several places. The only significant river in the northern desert is the Loa, which flows into the Pacific Ocean north of the Atacama. South of the Atacama, the land is less arid. Several rivers—including the Copiapó, Huasco, and Elqui—flow across the region. Some of these rivers are dry for part of the year.

The Elqui River near Vicuña flows through the valley where the Nobel Prize-winning poet Gabriela Mistral was born. She described the Elqui River Valley as "confined yet lofty, many-sided yet simple, rustic yet a mining area." Although many of Chile's rivers are of limited value for navigation, they are important for irrigation and for hydroelectric power.

The Central Valley

About 75 percent of Chile's population lives in the fertile Central Valley. This area stretches from the Aconcagua River, 50 miles north of Santiago, south to Puerto Montt—a distance of about 600 miles. This beautiful valley, which was formed by sediments washed down from the Andes, is rich in mineral nutrients, making it well suited to farming and cattle raising.

Several important rivers—including the Maipo, Maule, Itata, and Bío-Bío—traverse the Central Valley before emptying into the Pacific. Flanked by broad plains, the rivers water farmlands that are dotted with major Chilean cities. Santiago, Chile's capital, is located on the Mapocho River. South of Santiago, the fertile and level farmlands extend without interruption to the city of Concepción. Elsewhere the val-

Rugged coastal beauty distinguishes Viña del Mar, one of South America's foremost resorts. Steep bluffs that rise from the sea provide excellent views of the water.

A cable car climbs San Cristóbal, a large hill overlooking Santiago. Founded in 1541 by Pedro de Valdivia, Santiago is the fifth largest city in South America, with a population of 4.3 million.

leys of the rivers that flow into the Pacific are separated by low mountain ranges that are ridges of the Andes.

Beyond the Bío-Bío River, on the southern edge of the Central Valley, lies Chile's Lake Country—often called South America's "Little Switzerland." The area abounds with snowcapped peaks, sparkling blue lakes, pine-covered slopes, and mountain streams stocked with trout and other game fish.

The Archipelago

The Archipelago—a region of hundreds of islands that actually are the tips of mountains submerged in the ocean—stretches south for 1,000 miles, from Puerto Montt

Renowned for their scenic beauty, Chile's lakes offer boating, fishing, and swimming in cool waters surrounded by sand beaches.

to Cape Horn. Toward the east of this region the Andes decrease in elevation, though even in southernmost Chile, peaks rise to more than 6,000 feet. Along the coast are several lesser mountain ranges, whose peaks rarely exceed 6,000 feet.

The coast of southern Chile is cold and rain-swept. Massive walls of granite form fjords (narrow inlets of the sea between cliffs), and glaciers break off thunderously into the sea. Some of the stone terraces along the shore have bluffs over 2,000 feet high, which leave few places for ships to land.

Offshore, Chile fronts on some of the world's deepest ocean waters. Because of

Because Chile lies in a geologically unstable zone, earthquakes often occur with devastating results. On March 3, 1985, a severe quake struck central Chile—including Santiago and the seaports of Valparaíso and San Antonio—killing 177 people and affecting almost one million people. This family is beginning the task of rebuilding in a badly damaged section of Santiago.

the action of the area's continental plates, which knock against each other beneath the surface of the earth, Chile is frequently—and sometimes severely—shaken by earthquakes. The quakes have exacted a heavy toll in damage and in human life throughout Chile's history.

Southernmost Chile is a twisted maze of inlets, peninsulas, and islands. The town of Punta Arenas lies far south, on the Strait of Magellan. For most of its history the town has been populated by sheep herders, who graze their flocks on the nearly barren pastures. The discovery of oil near Punta Arenas in 1945 brought workers who settled permanently in the town.

The strait itself—a narrow passageway of water—was discovered accidentally by the Portuguese explorer Ferdinand Magellan in 1520, when his ships were blown through the passageway by severe winds. Only after the storm had passed did Magellan and his crew realize that they had rounded the southern tip of the South American continent. The twisting, 350-mile strait has been used ever since by ship captains to avoid going through the even more perilous and stormy seas around the island of Cape Horn farther south.

Cape Horn lies to the south of Tierra del Fuego (Land of Fire). An island, Tierra del Fuego was named by early explorers who, on a passage through the Strait of Magellan, saw the fires built by native Indians to keep warm. Situated at the southernmost tip of the continent, the steep, barren rock known as Cape Horn rises 1,391 feet out of the sea. The cape, which is usually cloaked in fog and lashed by winds and freezing rains, was named by Dutch explorer Willem Schouten, who discovered it in 1616 and named it after Hoorn, the town of his birth.

Climate

Chile is located mainly in the temperate zone south of the equator, where its seasons are opposite those of the Northern Hemisphere. In the Central Valley, where

Independent Picture Service

Southern Chile's many tiny islands, which are actually the peaks of submerged mountains, resemble the fjords of Norway. Here, cattle graze on the damp, grassy banks of a river in southern Chile.

15

The bougainvillea, a flowering vine named for the French navigator Louis-Antoine de Bougainville, is native to South America. Many Chileans grow the flower as a porch ornament.

and rainy all year, with temperatures in Puerto Montt averaging 59° F in January and 46° F in July. Rainfall in some southern areas exceeds 200 inches annually.

Flora and Fauna

Because mountain barriers isolate Chile, the country's flora and fauna have evolved differently from the vegetation and animal life on the rest of the continent. Wildlife is not as abundant in Chile as it is in other South American countries. Llamas, alpacas, and vicuñas—all humpless relatives of the camel—roam the northern plateaus. Wool from these animals is spun into beautiful garments.

The chinchilla, a small rodent famous for its soft fur, is nearly extinct because it has been over-hunted. A similar fate threatens the puma, the guanaco (also related to the camel), and the guemul—a type of deer native to Chile and prominently inscribed on the country's coat of arms. Among

most Chileans live, the days are warm and the nights are cool, with mild, rainy winters (June through August) and dry summers (December through February). In Santiago temperatures rarely reach the freezing point during the winter, though it can often be cold and damp. During the winter month of July, the temperature averages 69° F. In the summer, temperatures in the capital city rarely exceed 84° F.

The climate in Chile's northern desert is cool compared to other deserts. The moderate temperatures are the result of the Peru Current, which flows northward along the coast, as well as of the cool air that circulates down from the Andes along the eastern border. Temperatures in this region average 69° F in January and 57° F in July. In southern Chile it is cool, windy,

The copihue, Chile's national flower, grows wild throughout the Temuco region from October to July. The plant blooms in shades of vibrant red, delicate pink, or snowy white.

Araucarias, or monkey puzzle trees, grow in the Chilean Andes. These evergreens grow straight and are free from knots, making them valuable for their beautifully veined hardwood as well as for their plentiful resin. Lumber, pulp, and paper are produced from Chile's annual timber cut.

Both the alpaca (right) and the vicuña (left) are closely related to the llama. Although llamas are used as beasts of burden, the alpaca and vicuña are kept mostly for their plentiful wool, which is woven into a very fine cloth.

other animals still found in the wild are the Andean wolf and the spike-horned pudu—the smallest known deer—which stands only 12 to 13 inches high.

In contrast to the scarcity of wildlife on land, Chile's Pacific waters are well endowed with more than 200 species of fish. The fish thrive along Chile's shores, which are cooled by Antarctic waters carried up the country's coast by the Peru Current. Many of these fish, such as tuna, are commercially valuable. Chile is one of the world's most important fishing nations. Its expanding fleets catch nearly four million tons of fish each year.

The country's winged creatures include the condor, albatross, pelican, cormorant, gull, swan, duck, parrot, and several kinds of hummingbirds. Many game birds that are long extinct elsewhere in the world continue to flourish in Chile—a mystery that naturalists have yet to explain.

Chile's national flower, a splendid lily, thrives in many areas of the country. Several species of cactus—some of which are found nowhere else in the world—grow in the northern desert. Varieties of peppers,

17

From the top of San Cristóbal Hill, the modern buildings of Santiago are visible. The Andes can be seen in the background, but they are sometimes hidden by clouds or smog.

beans, and corn are also native to Chile, where they were cultivated long before the arrival of Europeans. The potato, which originated in the Andes, still grows wild in Chile. South of the Bío-Bío River, forests cover the land. One of the most distinctive trees in this region is the araucaria, or monkey puzzle tree—a tall evergreen.

Santiago

Santiago is the capital city of Chile. With over four million people living in its metropolitan area, the city is home to one-third of the country's population, making it Chile's largest urban area. Situated in the fertile and productive Central Valley, San-

tiago's magnificent setting includes Andean peaks to the east.

The spacious city features several broad, tree-lined avenues and parks with landscaped gardens. Although numerous modern office and apartment buildings have been built, few skyscrapers break the horizon because of the danger posed by earthquakes. Many buildings of historic interest have been carefully restored. Some of the refurbished buildings house museums that display reminders of Santiago's long history, beginning with the city's founding in 1541.

Santiago is the seat of the government of Chile, which employs nearly 40 percent of the nation's work force. Government

The Mapocho River crosses Santiago from west to east and flows through an artificial stone channel spanned by several bridges.

The site of many castles, chalets, fine houses, and gardens, the famous resort town of Viña del Mar is located on the south central coast of Chile near Valparaíso.

employees staff the offices of large, government-owned enterprises, including the national railroads, development corporations, and scores of other government industries of national scope. Santiago also has many privately owned companies, which process much of Chile's agricultural output and manufacture everything from appliances to textiles.

The bustling cultural life of the city centers around three universities, whose students eagerly throng the city's concert halls and theaters. Many students are socially conscious as well, actively participating in political and community activities. Within Santiago many students are involved in programs to improve the quality of life among the city's poor, who make up an estimated one-quarter of the population.

Like other Latin American countries, Chile has undergone rapid urbanization in recent years. Most of the new people settling in the city come from rural areas and need help to compete for scarce jobs during times of very high unemployment. These newcomers often live in crowded, one-room shacks that lack running water, electricity, sewage disposal, and garbage collection. Chileans call these slums, which circle the city in ever-widening rings, *ca-llampas* (mushrooms) because they seem to spring up overnight.

Secondary Cities

West of Santiago lie Valparaíso (population 267,000), Chile's principal port, and Viña del Mar (population 316,000), the country's most popular seaside resort. It takes about three hours by train, bus, or automobile to reach these cities from Santiago. Valparaíso and Viña del Mar are just a few miles apart—a distance traveled in minutes by express buses and electric trains.

The port section of Valparaíso is a jumble of trading companies and commercial establishments that line winding streets built long ago on land reclaimed from the sea. In contrast, Viña del Mar (Vineyard of the Sea) is the tidy and well-groomed summer home of Chile's wealthy citizens. It boasts fine hotels and a magnificent municipal theater. Behind the city itself lies a large artificial lake where vacationers picnic, swim, and water-ski.

Most other Chilean cities are either ports or inland farming or mining centers. In the north, Arica (population 128,000) is a port near the Peruvian frontier, and farther south lie the ports of Iquique (population

Chile's rocky coast stretches for 2,650 miles along the Pacific Ocean and is about three times the length of California's Pacific coastline.

Antofagasta is the largest city in northern Chile. The port exports nitrates and copper and is the site of a Bolivian silver refinery dating from 1868.

121,000) and Antofagasta (population 175,000). All three cities trace their origins to mining and have become thriving centers for commercial fishing operations.

South of Santiago, the port of Talcahuano (population 221,000) serves Concepción (population 218,000), a city about 10 miles inland on the Bío-Bío River. Like Santiago, Concepción has a vigorous cultural life and a large and politically active student body at the local university. The city is also one of Chile's main industrial

Fishing boats are a common sight in Puerto Montt, and visitors to the region enjoy crab and other fresh shellfish.

centers, thanks to locally available coal, to hydroelectric energy from the Bío-Bío River, and to excellent road and rail connections with other Chilean cities and towns.

Inland, stretching down the length of the Central Valley, several more cities are situated at regular intervals. Each serves as a commercial center for surrounding farmlands or nearby mines and has a growing industrial sector. Rancagua (population 152,000) owes its importance to the proximity of El Teniente, the world's largest underground copper mine. Farther south, Talca (population 145,000) and Chillán (population 129,000) are situated in the middle of productive farmlands.

The city of Temuco is also surrounded by prosperous farmlands. Nearby live 20,000 Mapuche Indians, descendants of the Araucanians, who put up a stiff resistance to Chile's Spanish conquerors. The Indians sell their beautifully woven garments and crafts at the market in Temuco.

Photo by Amandus Schneider

Large palm trees (above) line a river in Viña del Mar. Beaches, bathing resorts, a casino, lakes, museums, racecourses, and parks contribute to the town's popularity as a vacation spot. In contrast, Valparaíso (below) is a bustling industrial port, where railways and ship lines meet to complete the connection between producers and markets.

Independent Picture Service

At the top of Santa Lucía Hill in the heart of Santiago is Hidalgo Castle, a colonial fortress whose cannons echo through the city streets at noon each day.

2) History and Government

Before the arrival of Europeans, the territory of modern Chile was inhabited by Araucanian Indians—fiercely independent warrior-farmers whose descendants have survived to the present. In preconquest times, most Araucanians were vegetarians. They supported their way of life by raising corn, squash, beans, and potatoes and by gathering and eating nourishing piñons—the nutlike seeds produced by several varieties of native pine trees.

The Conquest

Although they lived at peace with one another, the Araucanians stubbornly resisted any intrusion on their territory by outsiders. Before the arrival of the Spaniards, they had repeatedly defeated armies sent by the Incas, who came from the north to conquer them and to incorporate their lands into the Inca Empire.

When a Spanish conqueror, Pedro de Valdivia, entered their territory after a difficult march through the cold, rugged Andes, the Araucanians again mounted fierce resistance. With weapons more powerful than those of the Indians, however, Valdivia and his troops succeeded in establishing Chile's first Spanish settlement at Santiago in 1541.

Defeated in war but not in spirit, the Araucanians retreated to the south where they staged frequent uprisings. During

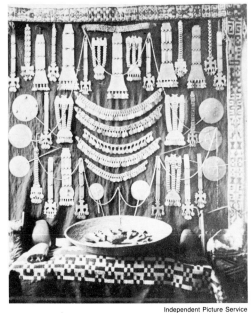
Present-day Araucanian Indians employ age-old intricate techniques in their careful silver work. In addition to crafting jewelry from silver, their ancestors also used gold, copper, and tin.

Independent Picture Service

canians make their peace with the government of Chile and agree to live on land grants south of the Bío-Bío River.

Spanish Rule

For more than three centuries, from about 1500 to the early 1800s, the colony of Chile was ruled by Spanish viceroys whose seat of power was to the north in Lima, Peru. Spanish rulers paid little attention to Chile, since—unlike Peru—the colony produced little gold or silver. As a result, Chile evolved quite differently from Spanish colonies to the north, where Spain imposed rigidly defined systems of government and control.

Chile attracted only the hardiest settlers, who, with little government interference, developed the fertile lands around

one such revolt, Valdivia himself was defeated by forces led by the Indian Lautaro. Lautaro had earlier been captured by the Spaniards in their raids to the south, and Valdivia had made the young Indian his stable groom. But, undaunted, Lautaro escaped, after having familiarized himself with Spanish customs and tactics. On Christmas Day 1553 he returned with an Araucanian force and overcame Valdivia and about 50 Spaniards. Valdivia was killed, according to legend, when molten gold was poured down his throat.

Lautaro was later killed in battle, becoming the martyr of Araucanian resistance, which would continue for over three centuries and would cost more than 50,000 Spanish lives. The legend of Lautaro is the theme of the epic poem *La Araucana,* written by Alonso de Ercilla y Zúñiga, a Spanish soldier and poet who kept a diary of the warfare with the Indians. Not until 1883—long after Chile had obtained its independence from Spain—did the Arau-

Courtesy of L'Enc Matte

This statue in Santiago commemorates Pedro de Valdivia, founder of Concepción and Valdivia, as well as of Santiago. Born in Spain in 1500, Valdivia was killed during an Indian uprising in Chile in 1554.

24

In characteristic Spanish colonial style, this courtyard features a garden, a covered walk, a series of archways, a roof tiled in red clay, and brightly glazed ceramic tiles on the walls and on the basin of the fountain.

Santiago and then gradually opened up rich lands farther south. By 1700 the territory of modern Chile had a population of only about 100,000 people. Foremost among these inhabitants were prosperous farmers, who sold their surplus wheat and cattle to the more heavily populated colony of Peru.

Like other Spanish colonies, Chile was forbidden to trade with nations other than Spain. Nevertheless, Chilean entrepreneurs commonly engaged in commerce with traders from several nations. Dutch and British ships, for example, regularly anchored

Dating from the seventeenth century, the Church of San Francisco in Santiago is one of the city's oldest buildings. The iron-grilled windows and deeply carved, massive wooden doors typify Spanish colonial architecture.

25

A Spanish defensive tower in the town of Valdivia dates from the eighteenth century. Warfare between the Indians and European immigrants continued intermittently from the colonial period until the late nineteenth century.

Photo by Don Irish

at Chilean ports to exchange manufactured goods for the country's agricultural products.

Independence

As elsewhere in Spain's New World colonies, local people were inspired to seek their independence by the successful examples of the U.S. and French revolutions. When Napoleon Bonaparte invaded Spain and exiled the Spanish monarch, Chileans took advantage of Spain's weakness by declaring their objections to colonial rule. On September 18, 1810, landowners organized a *cabildo abierto*, or town meeting, in Santiago. Chileans proclaimed their independence at this meeting, and seven people were elected to a national council to oversee the transition of Chile from a colony to an independent nation.

Subsequently, in July 1811, Chile's first national legislative body was assembled. Among its members was the military leader of Chilean patriots, Bernardo O'Higgins, who is revered as the father of Chilean independence. O'Higgins was the illegitimate son of an Irish farmer, Ambrosio O'Higgins, who had achieved prominence in the service of Spain and who had

Courtesy of L'Enc Matte

Los Dominicos, a colonial-era church in Santiago, reflects the Catholic influence on the New World colonies.

Courtesy of Organization of American States

This sketch shows La Moneda, Santiago's presidential palace, as it appeared in the colonial era.

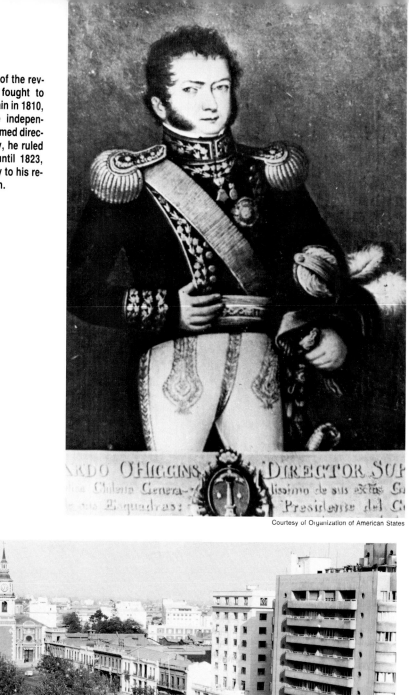

Bernardo O'Higgins, one of the revolutionary leaders who fought to break Chile's ties with Spain in 1810, proclaimed the absolute independence of Chile in 1818. Named director general of the country, he ruled with dictatorial powers until 1823, when widespread hostility to his regime forced him to resign.

Avenida Bernardo O'Higgins—a boulevard named for the first president of the republic—is 325 feet wide. Lined with trees, gardens, fountains, and statues, the thoroughfare is also called the "Avenue of Delights." At one time this street was the bed of the Mapocho River, but because of frequent floodings the river was rechanneled so that the roadway could be built.

Independent Picture Service

Argentine liberator José de San Martín joined forces with Bernardo O'Higgins to defeat the Spanish and to establish a nationalist government in Chile in 1818. San Martín refused the Chilean presidency, offering it instead to O'Higgins, his lieutenant. In 1820 San Martín went on to liberate Peru, where he was named protector of the country.

risen to the positions of captain general of Chile and viceroy of Peru. Although the father had little direct contact with his son, he saw to it that Bernardo received a good education in Great Britain. Following his father's death, Bernardo returned to Chile where he was at once drawn into the struggle for independence.

BERNARDO O'HIGGINS

O'Higgins distinguished himself in battle in a joint effort with the Argentine liberator José de San Martín. Together they defeated Spanish forces that had marched down from the north to reassert control over Chile. The Spanish were beaten in 1817 at the Battle of Chacabuco, midway between Santiago and the pass over the Andes to Argentina. The following year, O'Higgins, with San Martín's support, set

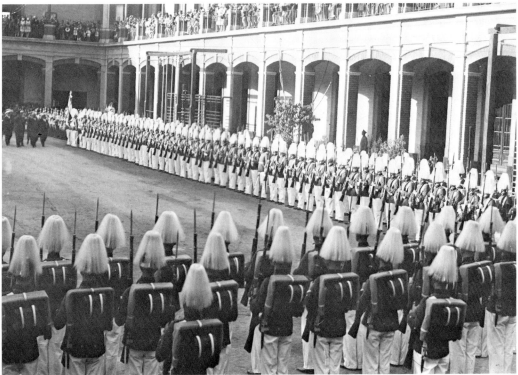

Independent Picture Service

Called the "West Point of Chile," the Military Academy in Santiago was founded in 1817 and is maintained by the government. This review of cadets demonstrates the high standards of training and discipline for which the Chilean armed forces are noted.

Artwork by Jim Simondet

Adopted in 1817 and designed by Charles Wood, a U.S. volunteer in the Chilean army, the Chilean flag is based on the design of the flag of the United States. The red symbolizes the blood shed in the country's struggle for independence; the white represents the snows of the Andes; and the blue stands for the sky. The white star, which was a symbol used by the native Indians long before the arrival of the Spanish, represents the progress and honor of the nation.

up a temporary constitution for the new nation of Chile and became the country's supreme director.

From 1817 to 1823 Bernardo O'Higgins ruled Chile with a firm hand. He angered some of the wealthy landowners by taxing them heavily to build roads and schools and by attempting to break up some huge farm estates as part of a program of land reform. To his deep disappointment, O'Higgins found resistance from several groups that disagreed with his priorities for changes in Chile.

Liberals charged O'Higgins with not moving quickly enough to create a fair society. Conservatives opposed any change that might disrupt the lifestyle they were used to. Clerics feared that O'Higgins was bent on weakening the power of the Roman Catholic Church. As opposition to his rule became organized, an open revolt erupted in Concepción, and O'Higgins voluntarily removed himself from the scene.

Disillusioned, O'Higgins sought exile in Peru, where he died in 1842.

Years of Development

Since independence, the nation's half million citizens had been sharply divided on constitutional and religious issues. Nearly 10 years after the departure of O'Higgins in 1823, Chileans finally agreed on a form of government that embodied their ideals.

When Chileans approved a constitution that represented their aspirations in 1833, however, the new nation acquired an enviable stability. Indeed, Chile's subsequent peaceful political evolution was unique among the former Spanish colonies of the Americas, most of which found early nationhood to be a period of bitter infighting for power. Chile had only four presidents between 1831 and 1871—each of whom served two consecutive five-year terms.

The first two chief executives were military officers. Joaquín Prieto held office from 1831 to 1841 and defended Chile from invasion by Peruvians and Bolivians. His successor was the victorious general of that military campaign, Manuel Bulnes, who presided over substantial economic progress from 1841 to 1851. With assistance from abroad, steamship lines were established, and Chile began to mine copper. Railroads were built, the telegraph was introduced, and foreign trade flourished.

Landowners, who had dominated the country since independence, were obliged to welcome into the power structure a new group of mining entrepreneurs, bankers, and businesspeople. Many of these people were self-made and were determined that future generations should enjoy the same opportunities that they had had. The University of Chile was established in 1843, and the government was pressured into investing heavily in public education.

INTERNAL TENSIONS

Chile's first civilian president, Manuel Montt, held office from 1851 to 1861. During his administration large numbers of German immigrants, mostly farmers, quietly settled the lands of southern Chile. Meanwhile, in the capital city the decade was far from peaceful. Montt, who proved to be more authoritarian than his military predecessors, faced civil war twice during his two terms in office.

Courtesy of L'Enc Matte

The Cathedral of Santiago flanks the western side of Plaza de Armas in the heart of the city. Although the cathedral still houses some relics from the colonial period, much of it has been rebuilt.

31

Two Chilean bills commemorate colonial-era men. Pedro de Valdivia *(left)* is imprinted on the 500-peso note, with the founding of Santiago at Santa Lucía Hill depicted on the back. Bernardo O'Higgins *(below)*, the "Liberator of Chile," and the arrival in Chile of Diego de Almagro—who led the first, unsuccessful Spanish expedition to Chile in 1535—are pictured on the half-escudo bill, a currency that is no longer used.

Government forces put down the first revolt soon after Montt's election, but a feud between church and state continued. In seeking to curb the power of the Church, Montt angered some of his own supporters, as well as members of the Liberal party who opposed him. The two groups united to form the Radical party, which would play a significant role in Chilean politics until the 1970s.

The Montt administration's repression of dissent led to a second revolt and several months of fighting in 1859. Peace was restored only when Montt agreed on the selection of a compromise candidate—José Joaquín Pérez—to succeed himself. Pérez ruled from 1861 to 1871 and enacted liberal reforms. For example, public services were improved and agriculture was expanded, particularly in southern areas of the country where European immigrants had settled in substantial numbers.

The War of the Pacific

By the time Pérez left office, however, Chile was feeling the impact of a global recession. In 1879 a quarrel with neighboring Bolivia over ownership of nitrate deposits in the northern desert erupted into the five-year War of the Pacific. Chile won a resounding victory over Bolivia and Peru and, along with it, ownership of the world's largest known deposits of nitrate, a natural fertilizer.

Beneath the surface of the newly won desert lay caliche, the raw material from which sodium nitrate is extracted. Farmers of the United States and other nations that produced surplus food were demanding huge quantities of this resource. With sodium nitrate fertilizer, they would be able to increase their harvests to feed a rapidly expanding global population. For

Various government administrations during the nineteenth century set aside funds to expand education, and learning became a respected pursuit. This statue honors José Victorino Lastarria, an outstanding professor who lived from 1817 to 1888.

Courtesy of L'Enc Matte

33

Chile, reliance on nitrate and, later, on other mineral exports would fundamentally change the context of Chilean politics, particularly as labor unions of miners developed political power.

Rule by Congress

Even though Chile's nitrate industry was controlled by foreigners—mainly British entrepreneurs—the nation's revenues from taxes on nitrate exports increased enormously over the next 40 years. The taxes supplied roughly half of all government revenues and enabled Chile to undertake a vast program of public works, including the construction of railways, port facilities, and government buildings. By the turn of the century, nearly 50,000 Chilean workers were employed in the nitrate industry. They organized themselves into trade unions that exerted an important influence on national affairs.

During the period of nitrate prosperity, presidents found it impossible to impose the old authoritarian style of government, finding it easier to bow to the desires of congress. Laws were enacted, for example, that curbed the power of the Church and that made civil marriages legal. Nitrate revenues were invested to improve public education.

When President José Manuel Balmaceda overstepped his constitutional authority in 1891, a short but bloody civil war broke out. More than 10,000 Chilean lives were lost in the fighting before Balmaceda was overcome. He committed suicide the day after his term ended.

Thereafter, political parties multiplied, which weakened the power of the central government. Strikes and labor violence

Courtesy of Suzanne Paul

Although the barren northern desert can support little vegetation, both Chile and Bolivia became intensely interested in the region after the nineteenth-century discovery of mineral resources beneath the soil.

The desert in northern Chile contains sodium nitrate, one of the richest of all plant foods. Mining and refining nitrate are complex operations. These men are using electric drills to make powder holes in the rocklike caliche, or nitrate ore, to ready it for blasting.

Thousands of Chileans have made their homes in the bleak northern desert, mainly to work in the mines and industrial plants. Large mining companies have established towns, such as this one at El Salvador.

This monument in Valparaíso honors Arturo Prat, a Chilean naval hero who fought in the War of the Pacific, which lasted from 1879 to 1884.

became commonplace, though Chileans enjoyed a free press and continued improvements in public education.

Economic Decline

Following World War I, Chile entered politically troubled times. International markets for Chilean nitrate collapsed because of the introduction and widespread use of cheaply produced synthetic fertilizers—the product of chemical laboratories in industrialized nations.

Amid frustration and controversy over a government that could no longer draw on nitrate profits to meet social and economic needs, Chileans sought new leadership. Arturo Alessandri Palma combined a natural gift for public speaking with personal appeal to represent the people's de-

sire for reform. Alessandri won the presidential election in 1920, only to find that his reformist program was blocked by opposition in the congress. When Alessandri tried to resign in 1924, the congress even refused to accept his resignation, granting him instead a six-month leave of absence. When Alessandri left the country, Chile's armed forces assumed leadership of the badly divided nation.

Restoration of Executive Authority

Upon his return to office in 1925, Alessandri drafted a new constitution, which was ratified in a national election that same year. The new constitution restored considerable power to the president and diminished the authority of the congress.

Alessandri was elected president again from 1932 to 1938. By then the champion of Chile's middle class and blue-collar workers, Alessandri presided over a strong

The 26-foot-high Christ of the Andes marks the boundary between Chile and Argentina established in 1903 after a 50-year dispute. The plaque reads, "Sooner shall these mountains crumble into dust than the people of Argentina and Chile break the peace they have sworn to maintain at the feet of Christ the Redeemer."

Chilean friends gather to socialize and make music at a rural home in 1928.

Courtesy of Organization of American States

regime that restored order in keeping with the new constitution. In reaction, the nation's Communist and Socialist parties were organized during Alessandri's administrations. With strong backing from organized labor, the Popular Front—a coalition of the Radical, Socialist, and Communist parties—won the presidency in 1938 by a margin of only 4,000 votes out of a total of 450,000 cast.

Under President Pedro Aguirre Cerda, this coalition moved quickly to direct the Chilean economy. The Chilean Development Corporation, a new governmental agency, was created with wide powers in the economic field. By the time Aguirre Cerda died in office of natural causes in 1941—just halfway through his term—he had become one of the most popular chief executives in Chilean history. He is particularly well remembered for innovative social legislation, including labor laws and welfare measures that benefited Chilean workers and their families. At the time of

Courtesy of Organization of American States

Central Station in Santiago bustles with activity in this 1910 photograph.

Although a parking lot now fills the front yard of La Moneda, the impressive changing of the guard once took place there at 10 A.M. every other day.

Independent Picture Service

Aguirre Cerda's death, the country was in general agreement that far-reaching changes were needed to create a more equal society.

Work toward that objective fell behind during World War II, when Chile was ruled by President Juan Antonio Ríos. As president from 1942 to 1946, Ríos, a fervent anti-Communist, broke relations with Germany and Japan and made Chile an important supplier of copper, nitrates, and other war goods for the Allied cause.

Political Disunity

When Ríos died in office, Gabriel González Videla—who had risen to prominence as a leader of Aguirre Cerda's Radical party—

won the national elections. Although González Videla—the minority winner—did not win a majority of the votes, he was confirmed as president by the congress because he received more votes than any other candidate. From 1946 to 1952 he headed a coalition government composed of Radical, Communist, and Liberal party members.

Within Chile, the division of people along ideological lines was widened further when the 1952 election again failed to produce a majority winner. Congress certified Carlos Ibáñez del Campo, a military officer who had ruled Chile dictatorially from 1927 to 1931, as the nation's new president. The aging Ibáñez, who was in his mid-seventies, proved unable to cope with rampant inflation and the rising tide of popular discontent. Chileans blamed foreigners who owned the copper companies for the nation's ills. They directed most of their dissatisfaction at the United States.

Jorge Alessandri Rodríguez, the son of former president Arturo Alessandri, succeeded Ibáñez. From 1958 to 1964 Alessandri sought to impose conventional solutions to pressing economic problems. At the same time, however, he initiated imaginative housing and agrarian reform programs in response to popular demands.

Promises to expand reform programs and to work out more profitable arrangements for Chile with foreign-owned copper companies helped Eduardo Frei Montalva win the presidency in 1964. Frei, the first Latin American president elected as a candidate of the Christian Democratic party, was also the winner by the largest margin in Chile since 1931—56 percent of the popular vote. As president from 1964 to 1970, Frei undertook an ambitious program of social and economic reform that he called a "Revolution in Liberty."

Salvador Allende Gossens

By the time President Frei left office, his own party had become divided over how reforms should be achieved. These dif-ferences contributed to the victory at the polls in 1970 of Salvador Allende Gossens, the first democratically elected Marxist to serve as head of state in the Western Hemisphere.

Although Allende did not enjoy majority support in congress, he immediately set out to transform Chile into a socialist state. He nationalized (converted from private to government ownership) approximately 80 major firms, including all of Chile's largest banks and industries. In addition, Allende nationalized the copper industry, which had been dominated by U.S. companies.

Chile's economic difficulties—aggravated by an economic blockade imposed by the United States—worsened. Inflation soared and widespread shortages sparked a period of strikes and violence, which was caused in part by undercover activities of the CIA.

Some people feared that Allende was determined not only to make Chile a socialist state but also a Communist one. With the Chileans divided on this issue, Chile's armed forces staged a military coup on September 11, 1973. Secretly supported by the United States, the coup resulted in Allende's death—whether it was murder or suicide is not known—and the deaths or exile of thousands of Chileans.

The Military Academy in Santiago not only trains soldiers but also houses displays on Bernardo O'Higgins, the Spanish conquest, and the War of the Pacific.

Courtesy of L'Enc Matte

On September 4, 1970, supporters surrounded Salvador Allende as he arrived at the polling station to vote in the election that made him president of Chile.

Independent Picture Service

Military Rule

Much as they regretted the bloodshed, many Chileans welcomed military rule. They hoped that strong leadership would end the economic and political disorder that had prevailed under Allende. The military junta that has ruled Chile through the 1970s and 1980s, headed by General Augusto Pinochet Ugarte, was initially favored because of a boom in the Chilean economy, which experienced an annual growth rate of about 7 percent during much of the 1970s.

Once in power, the junta dissolved congress and banned all political parties. The military also imposed a state of siege, which gave the government power to arrest, detain, and jail protesters without formal court proceedings. This measure was lifted in 1978, but the anti-Communist junta renewed the state of siege whenever it felt a threat to national security.

After coming to power, the Chilean junta ruthlessly repressed dissent and subjected political opponents to persecution, jailings without cause, and torture. Some prisoners were later released or were permitted to leave the country. Others disappeared after their arrest and are presumed to have been killed. Although Pinochet

adopted a new constitution in 1980 that called for a gradual return to democracy, many Chileans were impatient to have individual freedoms restored more quickly.

Courtesy of Embassy of Chile

Born in Santiago in 1915 and educated at the Military Academy, Augusto Pinochet Ugarte led an increasingly strong military dictatorship during his years in power from 1973 to 1989.

40

In a redeveloped area of downtown Santiago, the dark tower *(right)* and surrounding buildings contain offices of the Chilean government.

Courtesy of Museum of Modern Art of Latin America

During the 1980s the Chilean economy took a turn for the worse. With unemployment at historic highs and cutbacks in welfare programs being felt throughout the nation, Chileans became increasingly militant in demanding an immediate return to democracy.

The move toward reestablishing democracy suffered a setback on September 7, 1986, however, when 70-year-old President Pinochet was slightly wounded in an assassination attempt in which five of his bodyguards were killed. Subsequently, the junta again imposed a state of siege and proceeded to tap telephones, to open mail, and to hold prisoners at secret locations for reasons of national security. The Chilean junta also suspended constitutional

Independent Picture Service

Chile's supreme court—composed of 13 judges—convenes at the Palace of Justice in Santiago. Under military rule, the court has only limited power to decide on the constitutionality of laws passed by the government.

Photo by Don Irish

Despite the military junta's involvement in offenses against human rights, General Pinochet installed an eternal flame—symbolizing liberty—at the top of Santa Lucía Hill. Because opponents of the junta began to tamper with the eternal flame, it was moved to a more secure position beside Bernardo O'Higgins's grave in front of the Church of the Sacred Heart.

guarantees, banned public gatherings, and censored the press.

Governmental Structure

After the military coup d'état of 1973, General Pinochet led both the military junta and the army. Legislative authority was exercised by the four members of the junta, composed of the commanders of the navy, the air force, and the national police —called *carabineros*—and a representative of the army. All regional administrators, including governors, mayors, and university rectors, were appointed by the junta.

For administrative purposes, Chile is divided into 12 regions plus the metropolitan area of Santiago. These regions, in turn, are subdivided into provinces and municipalities.

In 1980, during a period of economic expansion, the junta called a national election. By a two-thirds majority Chilean voters approved a new constitution that provided for the eventual return to democracy. In accord with the new constitution, President Pinochet and his junta will continue to rule Chile until December 1989.

In late 1988 the Chilean people voted against giving Pinochet—the candidate nominated by the four junta members—an eight-year term as president. Although the outcome of the election surprised many observers, Pinochet accepted the results and agreed to call presidential and congressional elections within one year. After that, Chile's governmental structure could change considerably.

Although it was damaged by air attacks during the 1973 military coup, La Moneda, the governmental palace, has been completely restored. The building contains items of historical and artistic interest, as well as the elaborate Red Room, where official receptions are held.

Home to over one-third of Chile's population, Santiago serves the nation as the primary cultural, economic, and governmental center.

3) The People

Chile's 12.6 million people constitute an ethnically unified population descended from racial groups that intermixed during the colonial era. Mestizos—those of mixed European and Indian ancestry—make up more than two-thirds of the population. About one-fourth are European immigrants and their descendents, who are of primarily Spanish backgrounds. Members of Chile's Indian groups comprise about 5 percent of the population.

The culture, government, and business of Chile have been heavily influenced by the Europeans,. particularly the Spanish. Most mestizos have Spanish backgrounds, although some have British, Irish, and German ancestors. Italian, Yugoslav, French, and Arab immigrants also figure as small but important ethnic minorities.

In contrast to many other Latin American countries, Chile has an unusually stable population in numbers. A national commission to promote family planning has existed since 1974. Chile's annual population growth rate of 1.7 percent from 1970 to 1985 compares favorably with Western industrialized nations.

Population Distribution

More than 80 percent of all Chileans live in cities or urban centers. More than one-third of the total population resides in the capital city of Santiago. Over 90 percent

43

of the people inhabit Chile's Central Valley, with clusters of people living in and around ports and mining settlements as well as in the cities that serve surrounding agricultural areas.

Many of Chile's German immigrants have settled in the southern provinces, particularly around the cities of Puerto Montt, Osorno, and Valdivia. The country's surviving Indians, mainly of Araucanian descent, live isolated from the rest of the population on reservations south of the Bío-Bío River. A few Indians still speak the language of their ancestors as a second tongue, though the official language of Chile is Spanish.

Education

More than 90 percent of Chileans can read and write, one of the highest literacy rates in South America. School attendance is free and compulsory from the ages of 6 to 15. The country's teachers are well quali-

Built into cliffs that line the coast, Valparaíso challenges newcomers to the city with its many steep hills. The streets can be climbed by steps or by the *ascensor,* a cagelike elevator.

A statue of Andres Bello, noted author and statesman from Venezuela, greets students at the main entrance to the University of Chile. Founded by Bello in 1843, the university is one of the largest institutions of higher education in South America.

Many Chileans who attend the universities actively participate in the nation's political activities. Militant students frequently demonstrate on behalf of the increasing numbers of urban poor people, urging government authorities to provide slum dwellers with adequate housing and more jobs. Although the students differ on how these changes should be accomplished, they fill an important need in discussing these concerns. Under military rule, students represent the country's only tolerated opposition.

Health

Educational courses in nutrition and fitness are taught from the earliest days of primary school in Chile. Most Chileans

fied, and primary school classes usually are quite small, with only about 20 pupils.

A number of special schools serve the handicapped, and classrooms for the very poor are often located within low-income neighborhoods. Vocational training, which can take anywhere from three to seven years to complete, is provided at industrial and commercial secondary schools in urban areas. Agricultural schools in rural areas offer seven-year programs.

The higher educational system includes two public universities. The University of Chile and the State Technical University —both with branches throughout the nation—account for about half of the total university enrollment of more than 150,000 students. Of the 5,000 Chileans who study abroad, about one-fifth do so in the United States, and the rest study at European institutions. The most popular professions among young Chileans are teaching, medicine, and engineering.

At the Catholic University in Santiago, these students are preparing for careers in veterinary medicine.

A nurse inoculates these youths against preventable diseases – part of a national campaign to wipe out childhood ailments.

eat a well-balanced diet, and the country is self-sufficient in a wide range of nourishing foods. Recent years have seen a marked increase in the consumption of fish. Life expectancy at birth is 70 years among Chileans—a figure that approaches the life expectancy rates of Western industrialized nations. In Chile, as in other industrialized nations, the major killers are cancer and heart disease, and alcoholism is of growing public concern.

Except for the urban poor, most Chileans enjoy effective health care. Recent governments have placed an emphasis on innovative programs in the field of infant care and in the feeding of economically deprived children through government-sponsored school lunches. A surplus of physicians, dentists, and health personnel exists in the Santiago area. Authorities are encouraging some of these professionals to relocate to other areas of the country,

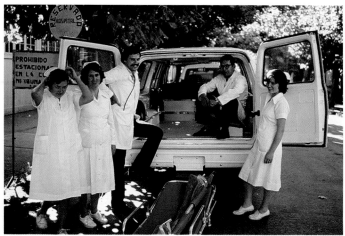

Chile boasts a well-developed system of modern medicine and emergency care. This first-aid team stands ready to respond to a call in Bulnes, a town about 50 miles east of Concepción.

where additional medical services are still needed.

Holidays and Religion

Holidays in Chile are comparable to those of other countries in the Western Hemisphere, with Christmas, Independence Days (September 18–19), Columbus Day (October 12), and New Year's Day all marked by family and community festivals. Chileans are much less given to the extravagant celebration of religious holidays than are the peoples of other Hispanic countries. For example, Holy Week (the week before Easter) is the occasion for just two holidays in Chile, in contrast to other Latin American countries that observe the whole week.

Most Chileans practice the Roman Catholic faith, though church and state were separated in 1925 and religious freedom is guaranteed. A number of Church-sponsored institutions—such as the Institute for the Economic and Social Development of Latin America—are active in Chile. More than 10 percent of the Chilean people belong to Protestant churches, whose memberships are increasing through missionary activities. Chile also has about

Photo by Don Irish

On one of the summits of San Cristóbal Hill in Santiago a statue of the Virgin Mary reaches into the sky. The hill is laid out with terraces, gardens, and paths and, at 985 feet high, affords a good view of the city.

A modern church in Santiago demonstrates continuing Chilean support for Roman Catholicism. Although the Constitution of 1925 separated church and state, eliminating Catholicism as the official religion, about 90 percent of the population is Catholic.

Courtesy of L'Enc Matte

47

30,000 Jews, most of whom live in the greater Santiago area.

The Arts

Chileans enjoy several well-established cultural institutions. The capital city of Santiago has three symphony orchestras, and Valparaíso and Concepción each have one. The Municipal Theater in Santiago—a regular stopping place for cultural groups touring the South American continent—is one of Latin America's foremost halls for ballet, opera, and concerts. The nation has contributed its share of performers to the world scene, including the outstanding pianist Claudio Arrau. Since the military takeover in 1973, touring groups of Chilean musicians—playing original works that criticize political oppression in Chile—have gained popularity in the United States. Many Chilean painters and sculptors also have attained international acclaim.

Two Chilean poets have won the Nobel Prize for literature. In 1945 Gabriela Mistral, a rural schoolteacher, became the first Latin American to be awarded this prize. Pablo Neruda, who served his country as a diplomat in the Far East and in Europe, won a Nobel Prize in 1971. Few political leaders of the past or present approach the popularity of Mistral and Neruda. Their verses are read by primary school students—and often are committed to memory. Even Chileans who are not particularly well read honor these two cultural heroes and quote from their verses on public occasions.

Chile has also produced many writers of lesser international stature. Since the installation of the military government,

Courtesy of Nobel Foundation

The first Latin American to win a Nobel Prize in literature, Gabriela Mistral was born in Vicuña in 1889. A noted educator as well as a poet, Mistral traveled to the United States and Europe to study schools and teaching methods and served as Chilean consul in several foreign cities. Her poetry has been translated into several languages, including English.

Son of a railroad worker, Pablo Neruda is considered one of the major poets of the twentieth century. In 1924, at the age of 20, Neruda had written *Twenty Love Poems and a Song of Despair*, which quickly became a bestseller. Neruda also served as a diplomat and was awarded the Lenin Peace Prize in 1971.

Courtesy of Nobel Foundation

A playful mosaic adorns a stone wall in Gabriela Mistral Park, located in Vicuña, the birthplace of the famous poet.

Courtesy of Suzanne Paul

Chilean artists, musicians, and writers have become extremely popular overseas as champions of Third World aspirations for social justice.

Sports and Recreation

Soccer, called *futbol*, is Chile's most popular sport, and stadiums are crowded to capacity for important matches. Soccer players attain the status of national heroes when Chilean teams perform outstandingly in international play. Basketball and tennis are also well-attended spectator sports. Some Chileans are avid horse-racing fans, and the nation as a whole takes pride in its carefully bred animals, which are among the world's finest.

A fitness fad has swept Chile recently, and many Chileans have become joggers. Public schools have excellent teams in track and field events, and youngsters often participate in bicycle racing, which is as popular in Chile as it is in France. During the winter, skiers from Chile and abroad flock to the Andean slopes. The Portillo ski resort is less than 100 miles from Santiago, and the Farellones and Lagunillas ski areas are less than 25 miles from the capital. During the summer

Courtesy of Organization of American States

About 85 miles from Santiago lies Portillo, the biggest center for skiing and winter sports in Chile. The resort offers many varied runs, excellent snow conditions, and ideal skiing weather from June to September.

49

Chilean rodeos test the skills of both horse and rider. Here, a boy and his father practice steer wrestling, in which they chase a steer around a semicircular ring until reaching a section that is padded in straw, where they try to pin the steer against the fence. If the steer is pinned by the hindquarters, the rider scores four points. Three points are scored if the stomach is pinned, two points for the shoulders, and none for the head.

Photo by José Armando Araneda

months, Viña del Mar attracts thousands of people from the Santiago area in search of sea, sun, and sand.

Fishing and hunting interest many Chileans. It is not uncommon to see parties of 20 or more departing early in the morning to hunt doves or to bag quail. Along the Pacific Ocean, resorts and local businesses feature fishing contests to challenge tourists, with prizes for catching record marlin and swordfish.

Chile has taken advantage of its abundance of beautiful scenery to establish parks at several locations in the Andes.

Courtesy of L'Enc Matte

At a beach near Viña del Mar, Chileans enjoy the ocean water and the rugged rock formations along the shore.

A market in suburban Santiago overflows with abundant fruits and vegetables.

Chileans enjoy camping at public parks or private campgrounds located in scenic areas such as the Lake Country.

Food

Chileans generally eat a light breakfast, such as toast—with butter and marmalade—and coffee, brewed with equal parts of dark coffee and hot milk. The day's main meal is eaten in the early afternoon. Tea and cakelike desserts are served in the late afternoon, while the last meal of the day is served in the evening between eight and ten.

In low-income homes, beans and rice are common foods, supplemented by cheese and fruit and occasionally by meat or fish. Thick soups of corn or rice, mixed with vegetables and chicken or other meats are also popular. Many Chileans drink locally produced wine with their main meal.

Among the middle class and the wealthy, the major meal of the day regularly features soup, meat or seafood, and vegetables, followed by dessert and coffee. Shrimp, swordfish, tuna, and conger eel are popular seafood offerings. Many national dishes combine meat with vegetables. *Cazuela de ave,* for example, mixes chicken, potatoes, corn, rice, onions, and hot peppers.

To make *cazuela de ave,* a Chilean national dish, pieces of chicken are fried and added to a stew along with fresh, chopped vegetables.

Copper miners line up in the morning to await a ride down into the mine at El Salvador.

4) The Economy

In Chile's mixed economy, the national government owns and operates approximately 70 percent of the nation's 100 largest companies. The state runs some of these companies—such as railways and utilities—by itself. Others are operated jointly with private entrepreneurs. Under military rule the Chilean government has sought to sell industries that can be more efficiently and profitably operated through private ownership.

Labor Unions

Chilean workers, with the backing of political leaders, began to organize themselves into trade unions in the early twentieth century. Since then, these labor organizations have become a vital and influential political force. They represent workers in the mining, oil, plastics, textile, railroad, sugar, and maritime industries. There are even organizations of public employees and of peasants.

Shipwrights work on the hull of a fishing vessel at the San Pedro shipyard in San Antonio.

Unions support the candidates of various political parties after the leading issues of the day have been debated. Despite heavy-handed efforts by Chile's military rulers to break up Chilean unions —on the grounds that they have become dominated by radical elements—the organizations have survived.

In 1981 Chile experienced the birth of a new labor confederation, the Democratic Union of Workers, which claimed 49 affiliated unions with a combined membership

Oil, first discovered in 1945 at Tierra del Fuego, has opened up a new and important industry in Chile. This refinery at Concón, just north of Valparaíso, processes thousands of barrels of oil a day. The growth of the industry has spurred the development of small boomtowns in the south.

53

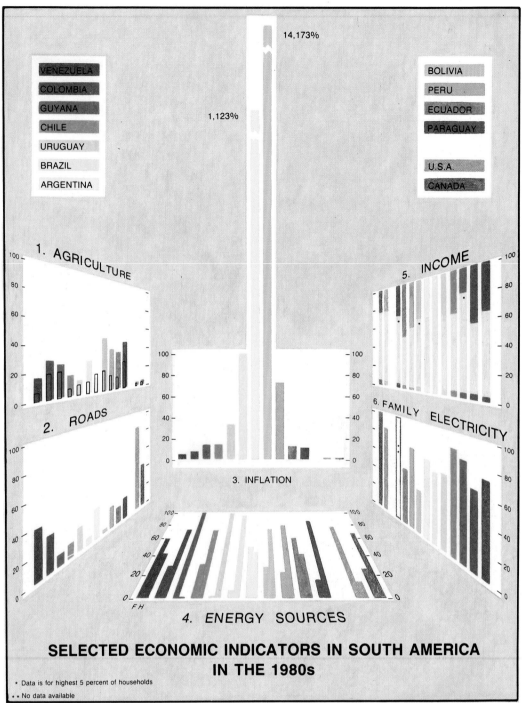

SELECTED ECONOMIC INDICATORS IN SOUTH AMERICA IN THE 1980s

VENEZUELA
COLOMBIA
GUYANA
CHILE
URUGUAY
BRAZIL
ARGENTINA

BOLIVIA
PERU
ECUADOR
PARAGUAY

U.S.A.
CANADA

14,173%

1,123%

1. AGRICULTURE

2. ROADS

3. INFLATION

4. ENERGY SOURCES

5. INCOME

6. FAMILY ELECTRICITY

* Data is for highest 5 percent of households

** No data available

Artwork by Carol F. Barrett

This multigraph depicts six important South American economic factors. The same factors for the United States and Canada are included for comparison. Data is from *1986 Britannica Book of the Year, Encyclopedia of the Third World, Europa Yearbook,* and *Countries of the World and their Leaders, 1987.*

In GRAPH 1—labeled Agriculture—the colored bars show the percentage of a country's total labor force that works in agriculture. The overlaid black boxes show the percentage of a country's gross domestic product that comes from agriculture. In most cases—except Argentina—the number of agricultural workers far exceeds the amount of income produced by the farming industry.

GRAPH 2 depicts the percentage of paved roads, while GRAPH 3 illustrates the inflation rate. The inflation figures for Colombia, Guyana, and Brazil are estimated. GRAPH 4 depicts two aspects of energy usage. The left half of a country's bar is the percentage of energy from fossil fuel (oil or coal); the right half shows the percentage of energy from hydropower. In GRAPH 5, which depicts distribution of wealth, each country's bar represents 100 percent of its total income. The top section is the portion of income received by the richest 10 percent of the population. The bottom section is the portion received by the poorest 20 percent. GRAPH 6 represents the percentage of homes that have electricity.

of nearly one million workers. Although Chilean moderates and conservatives continue to fear the political leanings of the unions, Chilean workers still organize themselves to press for improved employment conditions and for better benefits.

Copper and Other Minerals

Chile's mineral resources—the country's chief source of wealth—require immense capital investments and advanced technology to be used efficiently and profitably. Throughout much of Chile's history, foreign-based international groups—mainly U.S., British, and German companies—provided the capital and technology and marketed Chile's mineral production in response to global demand.

Because the coal mines at Lota are located underneath the ocean floor, underwater tunnels have been constructed for the mining operation.

Much of Chile's copper production passes through the port of San Antonio, which is located on the Pacific coast west of El Teniente.

The largest single copper mine in the world, the open pit at Chuquicamata resembles a gigantic amphitheater, two miles long, a half mile wide, and 1,000 feet deep. Long ago the Araucanian Indians worked this mine for metals to make jewelry and ornaments, many of which have been discovered in nearby tombs.

A complete railway system has been built in Chile's northern desert for shipping ore from the mines to the processing plants. This train of 14 cars—each weighing 45 tons—is on its way to a crushing plant.

Torn free from the desert, caliche (from which nitrate is derived) must be further broken up for loading. A very impure substance, caliche is composed largely of gravel cemented together by a mixture of soluble (dissolvable) salts, including sodium nitrate, sodium chloride, and sodium sulfate.

A giant dumper, or cradle, takes 30-ton carloads of ore and discharges them into a crusher for the first step in the nitrate refining process. During a series of crushings, the ore is reduced to one-inch pieces.

A continuous belt carries the crushed caliche to the loading bridge, which distributes it to concrete leaching, or dissolving, tanks for further refinement.

Holding from 7,500 to 12,000 tons of ore, these leaching tanks remove the soluble parts by passing a strong chemical liquid through the ore to dissolve the salts.

57

The nitrate solution that results from the leaching process is taken to a crystallizing plant, where it is artificially cooled. The wet nitrate is delivered from the crystallizing plant to centrifuges that remove the water, thus preparing the nitrate for granulation.

After the nitrate is granulated it is ready to be shipped out. In its final form, as shown here, it flows like sugar—a form that is very different from the original huge chunks of caliche.

With about one-fifth of the world's known copper reserves, Chile established the State Copper Corporation in 1967 under President Frei. This agency supervised large copper mines and processing facilities, some of which continued to be operated by foreign companies. In 1971 President Allende completed the nationalization of all of Chile's foreign-owned copper holdings, which at that time were controlled by U.S.-owned companies.

The Copper Corporation oversees the annual production and export of over one million tons of copper. Since the government takeover, Chile has processed more of its copper ore before exporting it, thus making it more valuable. Under normal market conditions, copper alone accounts for nearly one-half of Chile's earnings from its export trade. Chile has also developed other mineral exports to help relieve its dependence on copper. These include molybdenum, gold, and silver. Of special importance to Chile in this group is molybdenum, a metal that is highly resistant to heat and is in much demand for military, aeronautic, and space applications. Chile also exports sizable quantities

of lead, zinc, mercury, iron ore, coal, and nitrate.

Nitrate Boom and Bust

Historically, nitrate played an important role in the evolution of the Chilean economy and deeply affected Chilean attitudes on economic matters. Chile became the possessor of lands that were extremely rich in minerals as a result of the War of the Pacific. These included immense deposits of caliche, the raw material of sodium nitrate—the world's most important source of natural fertilizer. With British investment, huge mining camps were established in the Atacama Desert in the late nineteenth century. A situation comparable to a gold rush developed, and many Chileans left family and friends to settle in the mining camps, where they could earn much more from the nitrate companies than from other employers.

By the turn of the century, demand for Chilean nitrate seemed limitless. Farmers throughout the world needed fertilizers to produce more food to feed an exploding world population. As owner of the world's largest deposits, Chile worked hard to satisfy the new demand.

Chile's exports of 363,000 tons of nitrate in 1875 became one million tons by 1890 and three million by 1913. That year Chile's nitrate industry employed 53,000 workers. For nearly 40 years, nitrate exports alone accounted for half of Chile's earnings, and provided the capital to build roads, schools, and public buildings. Then, suddenly, the bottom dropped out of the world market. The introduction of cheaply produced synthetic substitutes for nitrate—which were developed by chemical companies in industrialized nations—replaced the natural product.

EFFECTS OF THE INDUSTRY'S COLLAPSE

The loss of the nitrate industry was traumatic for Chile. The miners were not the only ones to feel the impact of the collapse of the nitrate market. Its effects were quickly transmitted throughout the Chilean economy, influencing the affairs of bankers, lawyers, accountants, suppliers, and government leaders. Still studied for its lessons, the history of the nitrate industry shaped Chilean attitudes toward foreign exploiters of their country's mineral resources. The bitterness of the experience spurred the organization of trade unions and led ultimately to Chile's nationalization of all its mining activities.

Since then Chileans have concentrated on how the country can best exploit its mineral resources for the benefit of everyone. When oil was discovered in 1945 near the Strait of Magellan and Tierra del Fuego, for example, the Chilean government moved quickly to organize a state-run company to oversee the oil business. The company, which operates two small refineries, supplies about half of Chile's petroleum needs. To reduce its dependence on foreign energy, Chile has created governmental agencies to explore the country's hydroelectric potential and to develop iron ore and low-grade soft coal reserves.

Agriculture

Long before Chile developed its mineral exports, farming and livestock raising were the backbone of the nation's economy. These activities—concentrated in the 600-mile-long Central Valley—are becoming increasingly vital as Chile seeks to diversify its economy.

The Central Valley's level lands produce a wide range of crops, including wheat, corn, grapes (both wine and table varieties), barley, beans, sugar beets, and

Even though Chile's Elqui River Valley lies within the desert region, it is far enough south to be quite fertile, with peach and walnut orchards and orange groves.

Courtesy of Suzanne Paul

59

fruit. The export of fruit has become an important part of Chilean trade. Livestock graze on natural grasslands and account for about a third of Chile's agricultural output, including meat and dairy products. Cattle raising is also concentrated in central Chile, but sheep are raised in the extreme southern portion of the country.

Chile's poultry production has been modernized in recent years, but the nation has much to do to improve other areas of its agriculture. Recent governments—uncertain about the value of agrarian reform—have made only sporadic investments in modern farm equipment. Many cattle raisers have delayed spending money to improve their pastures because of fear that their lands might be taken over by the government.

AGRARIAN REFORMS

Fears of government intervention date to 1962, when former president Eduardo Frei passed Chile's first agrarian reform law, which was intended to eliminate the unequal distribution of land. The new law established the Agrarian Reform Corporation, which was empowered to take over abandoned or poorly used property, as well as land whose production depended upon costly irrigation works. By the end of the Frei administration in 1970, 8.4 million

Courtesy of Inter-American Development Bank

As part of a Western Hemisphere program to eliminate disease among livestock, a ranch foreman inoculates cattle to prevent hoof-and-mouth disease at a ranch near Quillota.

acres had been redistributed to landless peasants and small-scale farmers.

Under Salvador Allende, Frei's successor, agrarian reforms fluctuated and pro-

Independent Picture Service

Farm machinery is a major import item in Chile, and modern farming methods are beginning to take hold. Progressive farmers are acquiring tractors and, as shown here, using mechanical threshers to harvest and sort wheat crops, which are Chile's leading agricultural products.

Vendors peddle agricultural products in the streets of Valparaíso.

duction declined because farmers were reluctant to invest in property whose future ownership was uncertain. Many Chilean farmers who had farmed the land for generations abandoned their lands. The government tried to make up for the farming decline by encouraging small-scale farmers to form cooperatives so that they could better compete with larger holdings and agribusinesses.

Since the military coup in 1973, reforms have swung back to where they started. To raise agricultural production, the military junta has returned many farms to their previous owners and has sought to break up cooperatives by granting land titles to individual cooperative members. Nevertheless, some single estates or agribusinesses still encompass more than 250,000 acres. Recent figures indicate that nearly 70 percent of the land suitable for growing crops is controlled by only about 15 percent of the nation's landowners.

Manufacturing

Political uncertainties of the recent past have also slowed investments, which are needed to modernize Chilean industry. Machinery at many Chilean plants is outdated. Only recently have foreign investors begun to show a renewed interest in Chile, bringing in the technology and equipment that the nation needs for industrial expansion.

About three-quarters of Chilean manufacturing is concentrated in the cities

Many Chileans earn their livelihoods from seasonal agricultural jobs, such as harvesting apples at this orchard about 50 miles from Santiago.

Courtesy of Inter-American Development Bank

Workers pack grapes that have been converted to raisins by drying in the sun. The raisins will be exported to foreign markets. Sometimes compared to California for the variety of crops produced, Chile raises many grapes and has a thriving wine industry.

employ about 12 percent of Chile's workers. Domestically owned Chilean firms supply most of the country's paper, textile, food, beverage, and tobacco, as well as a growing range of appliances.

Fishing and Forestry

Within Latin America, Chile's fishing industry is second only to Peru's and is increasing in importance because of new investments. Among commercially valuable fish, large hauls of anchovies and sardines are brought in by Chilean fishing fleets. In addition, food processing plants are rapidly increasing their production of canned fish for overseas markets.

Some Chilean fishermen are now focusing their efforts on Antarctic waters, where krill—small shrimplike crustaceans rich in proteins and vitamins—are extremely abundant. Food processing firms are researching ways to process krill into fish sticks and other forms that are easy to market.

The potential of Chile's forests is also impressive, with more than a million acres in pine tree plantations, mainly on lands that have been carefully reforested. Trees on these plantations have reached full size,

of Santiago, Valparaíso, and Concepción, with the balance widely scattered throughout the country. Manufacturing companies

With its long Pacific coastline, Chile has great potential to expand its fishing industry. Nevertheless, the nation's total yearly fish catch is already ranked as one of the highest in the world.

Independent Picture Service

With over 18 million acres of natural forests, Chile promotes the processing and exportation of timber products.

and a government-run forestry corporation controls their harvest.

The development of natural resources on land and sea marks a shift in governmental thinking in Chile. Previously the nation had the unrealistic goal of creating huge, heavy industries, even though the country is small and technologically poor. In 1950, for example, the state financed the costly construction of the huge Huachipato steel mill near Concepción. Today, with sharply reduced world demand for steel, the mill is no longer profitable.

The Future

Despite its repressive internal policies, Chile has experienced an expanding economy. Since 1973, the government has converted state-owned companies to private enterprises and has attracted foreign investment funds. From 1976 to 1981, Chile increased its total output of goods and

services by 7 percent annually.

The country suffered a setback in the early 1980s, when global depression hurt export earnings, forcing Chile to borrow heavily from abroad. In 1985 Chile began a program to reduce its foreign debt and bring its economy under control—a requirement for obtaining financial assistance from the International Monetary Fund (IMF). Under the IMF program, the Chilean government must lessen its financial support for essentials such as food and transportation in order to pay its foreign debts.

Although these measures have slowed the nation's economic growth, expansion has not stopped entirely. In 1986 Chile increased its output of goods and services by 5 percent and registered a $1 billion surplus in its trade. Maintaining a vital economy is one of the major challenges facing Chile as it also confronts the task of moving toward a more democratic society.

Index